JESUS is my SPECIAL fRIEND

WRITTEN BY SUSAN S. BALIKA
ILLUSTRATED BY VICKEY BOLLING

© 1982, 2003 Standard Publishing, Cincinnati, Ohio. A div   rights
reserved. Sprout logo and trade dress are trademarks of   tes of
America. Project editor: Jennifer Holder. Cover d
ISBN 0-7847

09 08 07 06 05 04 03

Standard
PUBLISHING
CINCINNATI, OHIO

I have a friend. His name is Zach.

Zach and I like to talk together. We wonder where clouds come from.

We plan rocket trips to the moon.
We share drippy ice cream.

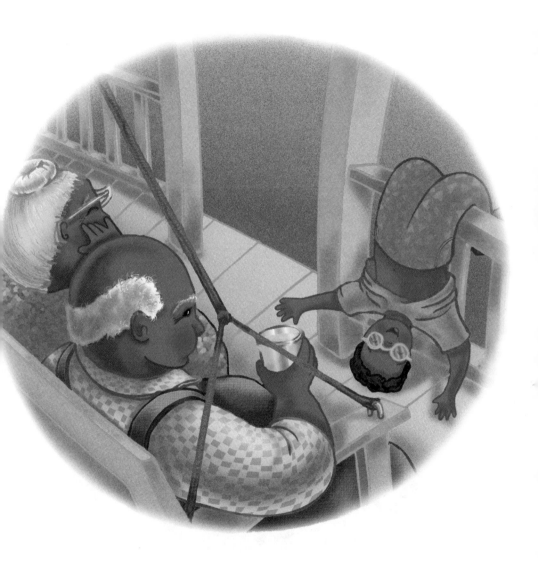

But sometimes Zach goes shopping with his mother. Sometimes he goes to visit his grandparents.

When we can't play together, I feel lonely.

I have another friend. Her name is Jamie.

Jamie and I liked to look at books and tell stories about the pictures.

We liked to color with bright crayons. Sometimes our mothers put our drawings on the refrigerator.

One day a moving van came. The moving men
put Jamie's books and crayons into brown boxes.

They took down her swing set. Jamie moved
away to another city. I miss her.

I have another friend. His name is David.
David and I like to play games together.

We build roads in the sand and make garages from blocks. We pretend that David is the mechanic and I am a race-car driver.

Sometimes we fight. We get angry with each other. David takes his big yellow dump truck and goes home.

That makes me feel sad inside. It is hard to say "I'm sorry."

But I have a very special Friend. He never makes me feel lonely.

He never moves away. He never goes home because he is angry with me. He is always with me, even though I can't see him.

He is with me when I lie on my back in the tickly green grass and look up at the clouds.

He is with me when I toss leaves high in the air and jump in the falling colors.

He is with me when I whoosh down the hill in the crunchy snow. He is with me because he wants to be with me.

When I've done something wrong, he lets me say "I'm sorry."

Jesus is my special friend. He loves me. He also loves Zach and Jamie and David. And he loves you! Jesus loves *everybody*.

Yes, Jesus is my special friend. He can be *your* special friend, too.